SOIL STEWARDSHIP HANDBOOK

FIDES VIVI HUMUS

Aaron William Perry

PRAISE FOR
SOIL STEWARDSHIP HANDBOOK

"Soil stewardship is not a partisan issue. It is essential to our society. As we each cultivate our victory gardens, we will establish the kind of liberty and grounded democracy that our forebears envisioned for us. This Soil Stewardship Handbook is an excellent tool for us to engage with this critical mission and quest."

—Michael Bowman
Founding Board Chair, National Hemp Association
and Chairman, *Hemp for Victory* Campaign
Founding Director, "25x'25"

"With his inspirational, aspirational, beautifully-informed and historically grounded handbook, Perry has given us a new appreciation for soil and its good works. Everyone who has ever enjoyed gardening will connect the dots as Perry reconnects us with an earthly wisdom that is as threatened now as the soil in which it dwells. This is an important little book that can be of immediate use to anyone who wants to help restore a greener Earth."

—Adrian Del Caro
Author of *Grounding the Nietzsche Rhetoric of Earth*
University of Tennessee, Knoxville

"I'm delighted to see the embrace of soil as a climate solution in the Soil Stewardship Guild. This handbook provides a nicely explained overview of the science with an inclusion of several easy steps that people can take to realize a regenerative future. Thank you for this contribution."

—Seth Itzkan
Co-founder, Co-director, Soil4Climate Inc.

First Printing January 2018
Printed in the United States of America

Soil Stewardship Handbook
ISBN: 978-0-9986294-1-4 (pbk)
ISBN: 978-0-9986294-2-1—(eBook)

Library of Congress Control Number: 2018901193

Earth Water Press
Denver Colorado
www.earthwaterpress.com

To book this author for a speaking engagement or workshop, contact y@yonearth.world

This book is dedicated to my two children, Osha and Hunter, whose brilliance, courage, determination and compassion give me great hope for the future.

This book is also dedicated to all other children alive today on Earth —of all ages—and the future generations who will follow us.

And this book is dedicated to the Y on Earth Community, the Soil Stewardship Guild members and the Community Impact Ambassadors who are informing and inspiring thousands with a message of joy, celebration, gratitude and deliberate action.

CONTENTS

FOREWARD

I hail from the verdant landscape of Europe's eastern Alpine region, where my people have lived for centuries in what is today known as Slovenia. Our land of glorious mountains, mysterious caverns, glimmering lakes, rolling hillocks and dancing meadows has been a cultural crossroads for millennia, and has in many ways remained a veritable Eden through the ages. In times of both peace and times of war, through epochs of great cultural upheaval as well as quiet interludes, my people have dwelled and thrived, nestled between the shores of the Adriatic Sea, the craggy Alps, and the great, fertile plains rolling down and away to the East.

My people love the land. We love the sea. We love the trees. And, we love the soil. It is, perhaps above all else, our connection with the soil that has preserved our countryside and that has allowed my people to flourish with a form of liberty that only exists through close connection to the living soil. In my culture, we have a deep tradition of family farming—virtually every family, from the youngest of children to the eldest of great grandparents. We connect to our soil within the loving context of family and within the steady rhythms of regular, day-to-day life. Gardening the soil connects us directly with the elements, the weather, and the continuous cycling of the seasons. Gardening the soil connects us literally and deeply to the living planet.

This *Soil Stewardship Handbook* is deceptively small and simple. For it is chock full of some of the most salient insights and a form of humble inspiration that are essential to these times in which we live. The book before you is a road-map of sorts, a guide, and a compass that will help set you on a path to great well-being and set us all on a path to regeneration, stewardship and sustainability on our Living Earth—Gaia.

We humans are now at a great crossroads, one characterized by immense complexity and intense challenges on mind-boggling scales. Challenges like rampant ecological devastation, staggering species loss, and climate change. But at this crossroads, we also find that the way through and out of these challenges include some of the simplest, most delightful, and most life-enhancing practices and habits we humans get to choose to enjoy here on Earth. In a world of seeming complexity, we will find that hardly anything is as complex as the living web of interconnectedness found in our planet's soil—trillions upon trillions of living creatures in each handful, interacting in beautifully sophisticated ecologies.

We have the choice to thrive and to heal—ourselves, our communities, and our planet—by connecting with the living soil, and by cultivating a deep awareness of the awesome miracle that is life on Earth. Respect and reverence will surely follow—which are necessary to take good care of this wonderful place upon which all of our lives depend.

I hope you'll roll up your sleeves, dive deeply into this *Soil Stewardship Handbook*, and dig deeply into the hidden memories of peace and abundance lying asleep within your body and soul. For you will find that, like my people in Slovenia, we are all living descendants of peoples who have long and beautiful traditions of connectedness to the land. We have to. For we are human, and being connected to land and soil is what it means to be human.

And now through our power of choice, we each get to choose to create the future by incorporating ancient wisdom into our modern lifeways. By planting, tending, reaping and celebrating the harvest—be it a single flower, or a great field of sustenance for hundreds—we have the choice, now, to cultivate our humanity and to heal our home.

We have the opportunity to reconnect with land and soil, to exercise our liberty as great steward-gardeners, and to cultivate a little slice of Eden—of heaven on Earth—right in our own backyards and neighborhoods.

Wherever you are, now is the time—dig in!

With Love and Hope,
Lily Sophia von Übergarten
Slovenia, 2018

NOTE FROM THE AUTHOR

Dear Friend,

I am thrilled and grateful that you have this *Soil Stewardship Handbook* before you.

As we explore in the *Handbook*, by cultivating a personal relationship with soil, we unlock the door to a vast realm of physical, mental and spiritual growth, health and vitality. We also join with millions of other human beings alive on the planet—right now—who are making THRIVING and SUSTAINABILITY a priority in their lives and communities as well. As this noble movement grows and develops, it will form the bedrock and will embody the guiding light of care and stewardship that will help us create a beautiful culture and future together—one marked by compassion, abundance, regeneration and wisdom. A culture of thriving and sustainability.

I want to personally welcome you to this individual quest and great global movement. We are embarking on an awesome adventure together—a fun-filled and health-enhancing adventure of a lifetime! By incorporating simple life-hacks and cultivating soil stewardship practices, you will enhance the strength of this movement, while enhancing your own health and well-being. You will get smarter, feel better and heal the planet—our only planet, our home, our Earth. The Y on Earth team and I hope you will join our Y on Earth Community, take the "Soil Stewardship Pledge" at the end of this book and help create the future we really want—a future that is right at our fingertips!

Gratefully in service and celebration,

Aaron William Perry
Y on Earth Community
Colorado 2018

SOIL STEWARDSHIP

"Find your place on the planet. Dig in, and take responsibility from there."
—Gary Snyder

"Soil is the answer. We are asking many questions on this journey together. Questions about our lives, our health and well-being, and about the sustainability of our planet. We will discover that soil is the answer to so many of these questions."
—Y on Earth

"What we do to the soil, we do to ourselves."
—Vandana Shiva

WHY SOIL STEWARDSHIP?

PURPOSE: The purpose of this *Soil Stewardship Handbook* is to help **you** THRIVE by becoming smarter and healthier, while making simple life-choices that will reverse climate change and heal our environments and communities. The *Handbook* provides you an easy, approachable framework for THRIVING as an individual, while simultaneously engaging with a powerful global movement toward SUSTAINABILITY—for our planet, countless species, our human family and future generations.

WHY—WHAT'S WRONG? We humans need soil—each and every single one of us—regardless of ideology, nationality, race or any other apparent "difference." Our lives depend on soil. But, through modern chemistry, industry and "conventional" agriculture, we have been destroying Earth's soil with a chemical intensity and a cultural insanity that is imperiling the entire world. We must stop destroying soil. We must *heal* soil. And, we must become expert stewards of soil—each of us— if we are to create and enjoy a sustainable future together. Time is of the essence!

WHAT DO WE NEED TO KNOW? We humans are from the soil—both figuratively *and* literally. We are *of* the soil. Our relationship with living soil is essential and foundational to THRIVING and SUSTAINABILITY. Our connection with soil is key to emotional balance, physical health and mental acuity—literally. Healthy soil is also key to clean drinking water, climate stabilization and environmental healing world-wide. Through soil, we:

Enhance our intelligence, health and well-being—for mind, body and spirit.

Reverse climate change by sequestering carbon from the atmosphere.

Heal our environments—especially fresh water, ocean, atmosphere, and agricultural lands.

WHAT CAN WE DO?

*"Upon this handful of soil our life depends. Husband it and it will grow
our food, our fuel, and our shelter and surround us with beauty.
Abuse it and the soil will collapse and die,
taking humanity with it."*
—From the Vedas, Sacred Sanskrit Scripture, 1500 BC

There's a lot we can each do—and the *Handbook* presents a fun and easy framework to do it! We call it the Soil Stewardship Guild. By incorporating three basic life-hacks into our own lives, we begin our Soil Stewardship Guild[1] journey as "Apprentices." Then, as we progress through four additional practices, we reach an intermediate or "Practitioner" level in the SSG. After that, five more core life-hacks bring us to a "Master" level of expertise. Additionally, we can engage in many group activities to cultivate our experience and enhance our impact within our communities, places of work and neighborhoods—essentially expanding the reach and impact of our Guild work together. By choosing to join the global Guild movement, we will heal existing soil, create more living soil, cultivate community, and reverse climate change—all while enhancing our own health and well-being!

HERE IS THE BASIC FRAMEWORK—IT'S SO EASY TO GET STARTED!

APPRENTICE (BEGINNER) LEVEL

- **Compost**
- Grow House Plants
- Buy Food, Beverage and Clothing Products with Soil Stewardship in Mind

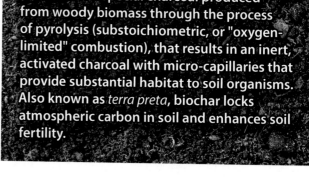

COMPOST is a nutrient-rich and biologically vibrant soil amendment produced through the natural decomposition of food waste, leaves, grass clippings and other plant-based materials. The process is made possible by a variety of detritivorous worms, nematodes, and micro-organisms.

PRACTITIONER (INTERMEDIATE) LEVEL

- Conserve Biomass
- Plant Gardens
- Plant Trees
- Use **Biochar**

BIOCHAR is a special charcoal produced from woody biomass through the process of pyrolysis (substoichiometric, or "oxygen-limited" combustion), that results in an inert, activated charcoal with micro-capillaries that provide substantial habitat to soil organisms. Also known as *terra preta*, biochar locks atmospheric carbon in soil and enhances soil fertility.

MASTER (EXPERT) LEVEL

- Connect with Soil Everyday
- Plant Garden Giants and Other Soil-Building Fungus Species
- Use Compost Tea, Bokashi and Worm Castings
- Use Biodynamic Soil Preparations
- Become a Soil Stewardship Guild Ambassador

COMMUNITY AND GROUP GUILD ACTIVITIES

These are the activities we can do in community, work and neighborhood groups:

- Create Compost Guilds
- Host Soil Building Parties
- Create Soil Installations
- Visit Organic Farms and Forests
- Establish Community Composting Programs
- Organize Tree Planting Parties
- Organize Soil Building Flash Mob Parties

By incorporating these personal life-hacks and community activities into your daily rhythms and routines, you will become a Soil Stewardship Guild member, and will join the growing ranks of one of the most noble and important movements of our time. We invite you to join the Soil Stewardship and take the Soil Stewardship Pledge.

SOIL—THE FOUNDATION OF HUMAN LIFE

"Ultimately, the only wealth that can sustain any community, economy or nation is derived from the photosynthetic process—green plants growing on regenerating soil."
—**Allan Savory**

We humans—our humanity—are so inextricably linked to soil, that describing this profound interconnectivity nearly defies words. It is strange that something so dear, so essential, can be so terribly taken for granted. Some of us might think we're merely talking about "dirt" here . . . that mundane, muddy stuff that gets under our fingernails, tracks on our floors and stains our clothes. Oh, but what an error of perspective this is! Soil is so much more than mere dirt!

REFLECTIONS & QUESTIONS

➡ How do you normally connect with soil?

➡ Do you compost?

➡ Do you have many houseplants?

➡ Do you have a garden?

➡ Do you plant trees every year?

➡ Do you deliberately touch soil with your hands every day?

➡ Do you connect with soil in some way at least once a week?

To truly see soil for what it is, we will come to understand that soil is cosmically sacred. Actually perceiving and understanding the magic, power and sanctity of soil will take our breaths away. It will augment our sense of awe for the Divine mysteries of Nature and Creation. It will change our lives. As our friends tell us in *Dirt! The Movie*, "Since the beginning of time, of all the planets in all the galaxies in the known universe, only one has a living, breathing skin called dirt." And it is upon this thin layer of Earth's living soil which all of our lives depend. All of us. Every single human being who has ever walked this planet—ever.

Soil is not just sustenance. Soil is essential.

Our histories and our ancient languages reveal this to us: in Latin, the words **humus** (soil) and **human** are closely linked. In the Hebrew of the Book of Genesis, **Adam** (humanity) is created from the **Adamah** (clay/soil). This creation story, revered in the Abrahamic tradition of Jews, Christians and Muslims alike, is shared by 5 out of every 8 people on the planet!

SOIL—ENHANCING INTELLIGENCE, HEALTH AND WELL-BEING

"Bring healing to our lives, that we may protect the world and not prey on it, that we may sow beauty, not pollution and destruction."
—Pope Francis

An awesome miracle of creation, soil heals us. By getting our hands in the living "dirt," we literally soothe the anxieties of daily stress, enhance our immune systems, and increase our production of serotonin—that "feel good" neurotransmitter that facilitates learning and causes us to experience joy. This is all made possible by the immensely potent effects of billions upon billions of micro-organisms—the **microbiome**—that inhabit each and every handful of living soil. Billions in a single handful! Think about that as the literal embodiment of life-force on our planet—life force we can each hold in our hands! We are just beginning to understand how complex interactions between the soil microbiome and our neuro-biochemistry enhances the growth of neurons and our overall cognitive performance. Our physical connection with living soil literally makes us feel better and makes us smarter!

Vibrant, living soil is also essential for the production of healthy, nutrient-dense food. By restoring agricultural soils to their natural, organic, and productively vital states, we will also enhance and restore the health—physical, mental and emotional—of humanity.

Soil is medicine—a very powerful medicine. Our friends in the scientific community are only just beginning to understand the miraculous ways in which our regular, literal, physical interactions with living soil enhance our health and well-being. As the micro-biome of our bodies—on our skin, and in our respiratory and digestive systems—interacts with the micro-biome of the soil, all kinds of amazing things occur. Our immune systems are boosted substantially. Our serotonin levels are enhanced. Our stress levels are reduced and our moods are improved. Those of us who are regulars in the garden and with the soil will attest that it even improves thinking and creativity. Some of us know from personal experience that some of our best insights, ideas and inspiration occur while we're connecting directly with living soil. We now also know through science that working directly in physical contact with soil also helps to alleviate the tension, anxiety, fear and depression of post-traumatic stress disorder (PTSD). The benefits are tangible and powerful! All of this from deliberate, regular contact and interaction with living soil. We have—right at our fingertips—a simple way to enhance our own health and well-being. By cultivating a direct relationship with living soil, we will THRIVE!

SOIL—HEALING EARTH AND RESTORING BALANCE

"A nation that destroys its soils destroys itself."
—Franklin D. Roosevelt

Over the past century we have been waging an all-out war on soil. Since the advent of modern warfare and chemical agriculture, we have been conducting a scorched-earth assault of global proportions on soil. Many of our poisonous chemical "inputs" used in this soil-destroying "agriculture" were developed by ammunition manufacturers during WWI and WWII. (Can you believe we would call this "conventional agriculture"?). Though extremely lucrative to the shareholders of these manufacturing companies, the planet-wide use of these poisons has led to utter devastation: severe soil loss and massive extermination of soil life. This deliberate poisoning of land also poisons water and air, as

well as our own bodies—especially through the consumption of contaminated food, the drinking of contaminated water and the breathing of contaminated air.

As a society, we have become soil-destroyers. And our destruction of soil now presents an **existential threat** to us all—old, young, black, brown, white, conservative, moderate and liberal—every single one of us. Living in a time when we have decimated and destroyed the life-force in soils all over the planet, it is critical that we understand this simple truth . . . and act on it. When considering what's good for soil, and what foods are good to eat, perhaps we should simply conclude that if a person has to wear a hazardous materials (hazmat) suit while spraying chemicals on the plants and soil,

we shouldn't be feeding ourselves or our families these foods! When assessing and debating emerging agricultural technologies and techniques, we should always ask ourselves: are they helping us build living, healthy soil? Are they being deployed with an ethos of stewardship, care and caution to advance the natural microbiology and microecology of the soil upon which we and future generations depend for our very lives? Is the soil healthy for us to ingest?

Right now, too much of our chemical agriculture is doing just the opposite.

But we can change all of this! Here's the thing—the good news, the hopeful truth: **when properly treated and cared for, soil is a renewable resource!**

We have so many opportunities to heal living soil—from large-scale, multi-national projects like the Great Green Wall of the southern Sahara region (an impressive, multi-national land restoration effort), to our own backyards and neighborhoods. The key is not the size of our soil-building effort, it is **that we simply begin it**—we begin to rebuild and regenerate soil. This sacred work is about reclaiming our role as stewards, and cultivating a humility and compassion grounded in utter gratitude for life on Earth—our own lives, each other's lives, and all of the lives constituting our living biosphere.

SOIL—REVERSING CLIMATE CHANGE

We need to get on (and stay on!) the path of deep carbonization! We need to grow natural carbon sinks—that means replanting forests on degraded land, reforestation and afforestation, and encouraging the soils to take up carbon!
—Jeffrey Sachs

It is largely through soil-building and ecosystem restoration that we will halt and reverse climate change. Yes, rapidly **de-carbonizing energy** as we transition from fossil energy to solar and renewable energy is essential to this global effort—we have to dramatically reduce the amount of fossil carbon we're releasing into the atmosphere.

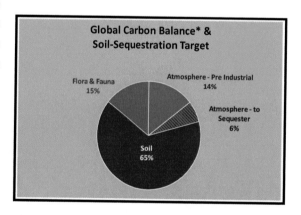

But we also have to understand that our energy production choices represent the lever that determines how much *more* fossil carbon we load into our already overwhelmed atmosphere. It does not resolve what to do with the excess carbon we've already emitted through our industrial fuels and processes. No. Even if we transition immediately to 100% renewable energy world-wide, we still have a situation in which the atmosphere is loaded with over 400 parts per million (PPM) of carbon dioxide. Carbon dioxide is a powerful "green house gas" that traps heat from solar radiation in our atmosphere and ocean. The pre-industrial "normal" level is 280 PPM. In other words, our human activity has increased the amount of carbon in the atmosphere by over 40%! Our critical task of climate-stabilization requires the reduction of atmospheric carbon, which is achieved by soil-building. We will reverse climate change by **re-carbonizing soil**—all around planet Earth! The amount of fossil carbon that we need to return to the ground is an amount equal to a 10% increase of the carbon content in soil world-wide. Just a 10% increase! Although it is challenging, and will

Earth Carbon Balance*	PPM	Billion Tons	% Total
Atmosphere Now	405	800	21%
Soil Now	n/a	2,500	65%
Flora & Fauna Now	n/a	560	15%
TOTAL		**3,860**	**100%**
To sequester atmospheric carbon, increase soil carbon by:		243	10%
* Excluding ocean and lithosphere			

require the combined efforts of millions of us, this is entirely achievable! This is within our reach, and this is our primary mission in the Soil Stewardship Guild.

If we look at the amount of carbon released to the atmosphere since the dawn of the industrial age—from the burning of fossil fuels as well as the destruction of agricultural, forest and native ecologies—we will see that we've increased the atmospheric concentration of carbon by some **243 billion tons**. That's a whole lot of carbon! Consider the magnitude of this: 243 billion tons is equivalent to burning 2.43 billion train car loads of coal—if made into a single train, it would wrap around the circumference of the Earth 1,017 times! But, because in the biosphere's overall carbon cycle, most of the carbon—by a long shot—is in the soil already;[2] we're only talking about an increase of soil carbon of about 10%. It's not necessarily easy to do. But it's entirely feasible. And that's key for us to really understand and embody—**we can reverse climate change** by collaborating with Earth's living systems to rebuild soil. And, as millions of humans world-wide engage in this urgent work together, we will each be a part of the biggest party that our species has ever experienced together on Earth! Now that's a party not to miss!

SOIL-BUILDING EXPLAINED: PRACTICAL AND AWESOME!

But what does it mean, exactly, to build soil? Soil building is a natural process, a continuous cycle that has been in motion for hundreds of millions of years on Earth. Because we humans have destroyed so much soil, and have emitted so much fossil carbon into the atmosphere, it is imperative that we collaborate with nature in order to accelerate the natural soil building cycle, heal our environment, and reverse climate change.

The soil-building process is one of the most complex processes on Earth. Despite all of our advanced technology, we are just beginning to understand the incredible sophistication present and alive in soil ecologies all over the planet. The good news, however—essential news—is that we don't have to totally understand the mechanisms in order to be expert soil builders, working alongside Mother Nature. The key is the micro-biome: the trillions upon trillions of tiny, living bacteria and fungus that interact with plant roots, worms, nematodes and other tiny animals, atmosphere, water, and minerals in a beautiful soil-building orchestra. Our job is to help them in their work. This means to provide exceptional habitat, nourishment and substrate (substances like biochar, **compost tea, bokashi** and **worm castings**), and to make and spread compost—essentially amplifying the work of the micro-biome.

COMPOST TEA is an aqueous soil amendment and foliar spray made by "steeping" finished compost in spring, creek or pond water (non-chlorinated water is recommended).

WORM CASTINGS are the excrement of earthworms. Over 1 million worms may exist in one acre of healthy soil, producing 700 pounds of enzyme-rich castings per day. They are a very nutrient rich organic soil amendment.

BOKASHI is a traditional Japanese probiotic liquid soil amendment made from in-vessel anaerobic fermentation of organic fruit and grain waste.

As the soil microbiome magically does its soil-building work, it not only enhances plant growth (which itself sequesters atmospheric carbon—locking it up in the wood of tree trunks and other biomass), it also collaborates with the plants to put carbon into the soil substrate in their root zones.

This is the amazing, mysterious, sacred soil-building process upon which all of our lives depend, and upon which the sustainable future of our species and civilization now depends entirely. We are on the edge of a very precarious cliff—some would say we've already gone over the cliff—but there's the possibility of a great safety rope here. An incredible safety net that we can deploy and utilize by building soil in humble collaboration with Mother Nature.

Time is of the essence—and we're all needed in this great, world-wide endeavor.

Are you ready to join and be a powerful participant in one of the greatest movements ever experienced?

Are you ready to build soil?

SOIL STEWARDSHIP—A JOURNEY TO MASTERY

The process that turns garbage into a garden is central to our survival. We depend on dirt to purify and heal the systems that sustain us.
—Peter Girguis

We start with composting. This "closing of the loop" of organic nutrients is a critical and necessary starting point. Those peels and scraps from preparing dinner? Soon to be soil! Those leaves that have fallen and are now blowing about the yard—ship them to the landfill? Heck no—they are a wonderful boost to your compost in the late autumn (or even early spring)—a wonderful source of carbon! Grass clippings? (First of all, let's shrink the sizes of our lawns and increase the sizes of our gardens!)—They are an excellent source of fresh nitrogen for the compost pile!

By growing plants in our homes, schools and work spaces, we fill these spaces (where we spend so many hours each day!) with vitalizing life force. The plants work unceasingly to purify the air we breathe, while also transmitting healing and stress-reducing life-force energy.

> **REFLECTIONS & QUESTIONS**
>
> ➡ How many living plants would you like to have in your home?
>
> ➡ What are you most excited to plant in your garden?
>
> ➡ What public space in your community is ideal for a living soil installation?
>
> ➡ Who among you and your friends would be great at leading soil-building and tree-planting parties?
>
> ➡ What level of achievement do you plan to attain in the Soil Stewardship Guild?

As we understand the power of our consumer demand—in particular through our daily food and beverage choices and our clothing purchases—we realize our impacts all over our planet, on soils, people, and Earth's ecosystems. This is the massively-scaling reach of the power of our intention and choice.

Then, utilizing a variety of life force enhancing soil boosters, like worm castings, bokashi tea, compost tea, biodynamic soil prep and biochar, we help nature super-charge her soil-building activities. **Worm castings** are the excrement of earth worms and an amazingly enzyme-rich soil builder—they are an incredible ally to the soil building guild! **Bokashi** is a probiotic cocktail brewed from organic fruit and grain waste, originating in the traditional agriculture of Japan. **Compost tea** is made by soaking compost in rain water, spring water or creek water, producing an amazingly bio-active and nutrient-rich aqueous solution that can be applied to soil. **Biodynamic soil prep** is a very specially formulated, super-life-force-charged probiotic admixture of composted plants and manures that is specially prepared in the Biodynamic tradition, and has amazing soil-boosting qualities. **Biochar** is a special form of charcoal that enhances water retention in soil, provides incredibly vast surface areas and habitat (at a micro scale) for soil organisms, and

> **BIODYNAMIC AGRICULTURE is a spiritual system of organic farming and gardening created by Rudolf Steiner. It observes planetary cycles, works with elemental energies, and involves the production of special soil preparations.**

locks up carbon in the soil that was just in the atmosphere a few years or even months prior. Biochar is key to putting climate-changing greenhouse gases from generations of fossil fuel emissions back down into the ground where it belongs!

But this isn't just about the direct benefits to humanity through the regeneration and stewardship of soil. This is also about our sacred role as stewards of our miraculous planet: Earth—our home.

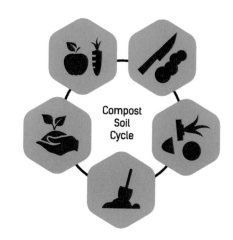

As we become expert in our regeneration and stewardship of soil—in our own homes, and on larger regional scales too—we will directly enhance the healing of water, air, and environmental habitat for all of Earth's creatures. We will literally heal Earth while we heal ourselves.

Composting is key. When we throw away kitchen scraps, paper and other organic, biodegradable "waste" it ends up in landfills where anaerobic decomposition releases more greenhouse gases like methane—exacerbating climate change. There is actually no such thing as "away"! Alternatively, when we compost those same carbon-rich resources in our own homes, offices and neighborhoods, instead of polluting the atmosphere, we build precious soil and create a special pocket of vitality that will enhance our gardens, landscapes and environments.

SOIL STEWARDSHIP PRACTICES AND LIFE-HACKS

It is easy to make soil a part of your lifestyle. You can choose to THRIVE with better health, stronger mental performance and greater well-being, all while helping to heal our world and to reverse climate change through these simple practices. Start today with Apprentice level life-hacks, then work your way through the Practitioner level and reach the Master level of the Soil Stewardship Guild:

INDIVIDUAL SOIL STEWARDSHIP PRACTICES

1. **COMPOST (Apprentice Level)**—Make or acquire a compost bin. Compost your kitchen scraps and other bio-based "waste" resources like paper towels and tissues—attempt to compost all of them! This way you are building soil instead of exacerbating climate change by causing more landfill emissions.

2. **GROW HOUSE PLANTS (Apprentice Level)**—Bring soil and living energy into your home! You'll improve the air quality, enhance the chi/life-force, and have amazing foods, medicines and herbs at the ready—along with soil ready for you to dig in at any moment—even when it's really cold outside! Spider Plants (*Chlorophytum comosum*), Aloe (*Aloe vera*), Day Lily (*Hemerocallis*), Snake Plants (*Sansevieria trifasciata*) and Dracaenae (*Dracaena marginata*) are highly recommended!

3. **STEWARD THROUGH CHOICE (Apprentice Level)**—Every time we buy a food item, beverage, or piece of clothing, we are directly impacting soil somewhere in the world. Often dozens of times per day! Choose organic, biodynamic, and soil-regenerating products—they're better for you and for our planet Earth! (Used and recycled clothing are a great option too!).

4. **PLANT TREES (Practitioner Level)**—Plant as many trees as possible, especially non-invasive, fast growing species that are well suited to your area! Learn which can be planted (or started indoors) each season of the year—Spring, Summer, Autumn and Winter!

5. **CONSERVE BIOMASS (Practitioner Level)**—In the autumn, keep all of those beautiful leaves in the landscape! Either leave them be where they fall to naturally enhance and protect soil, or rake and compost over-winter in your compost bin—whatever you do, save this precious resource!

6. **USE BIOCHAR[3] (Practitioner Level)**—Make or buy biochar for your houseplants, gardens, yards and neighborhood parks. You will enhance soil while reversing climate change by sequestering biochar's carbon, and providing excellent soil-microbe habitat for further biological soil building!

7. **USE WORMCASTINGS (Practitioner Level)**—Buy or grow wormcastings by introducing red-wigglers to your compost pile to enhance your soils with 106 powerful enzymes.

8. **USE COMPOST TEA AND BOKASHI (Master Level)**—Make or buy compost tea and bokashi. These natural liquid fertilizers are teaming with life, and will super-charge your plants, gardens and yards. Make compost tea by soaking compost in non-chlorinated water for several hours before spreading on your soil. Make bokashi by fermenting organic fruit waste and organic grain waste in an enclosed, aqueous environment.

9. **USE BIODYNAMIC SOIL PREPARATIONS (Master Level)**—Stimulate the elements, micro-biology and life-force in your soil ecology with these powerful preparations! Make or buy from a Biodynamic farm in your area or online.

10. **PLANT GARDEN GIANT MUSHROOMS AND OTHER SOIL-BUILDING FUNGUS (Master Level)**—The Garden Giant (*Stropharia rugosoannulata*)[4] is a magical species of mushroom that loves to be in your garden, that stimulates soil building, and that will flush a few times a year with delicious, edible mushrooms! As Paul Stamets tells us: "Mycologists can become environmental artists by designing landscapes for both human and natural benefit."

11. **CONNECT EVERY DAY (Master Level)**—Through a simple meditation, grab a small handful of soil from your garden or potted houseplant. Give thanks. Send love from your heart out to the world. Breathe deeply. Visualize light flowing over you and throughout the whole world. Heal. Be Well.

12. **BECOME A SOIL STEWARDSHIP GUILD AMBASSADOR (Master Level)**—Help others get started and succeed on their journey to soil stewardship mastery! Doing so will help reinforce your quest, your own learning and your own practice, and your humble leadership will be of great value to your community.

SOIL STEWARDSHIP PRACTICES FOR COMMUNITY

"The regeneration of our soil is the task of our generation."
—Ryland Englehart, Co-Founder Café Gratitude and Kiss the Ground,
author *The Soil Story*

The following community soil practices are great for neighborhoods, schools, places of worship and other community gathering facilities to engage friends and neighbors of all ages! Small groups of Ambassadors, parents, organizational leaders and community mentors can work together to plan, promote and facilitate these fun, enriching events:

1. **CREATE COMPOST GUILDS**—Collaborate with neighbors and friends to make compost bins, and to facilitate entire communities' composting of valuable organic resources.

2. **HOST SOIL BUILDING PARTIES**—Invite friends, neighbors and strangers to get together and make compost tea, biochar, and spread soil around the landscape—it's a great way to build community *and* reverse climate change!

3. **CREATE SOIL INSTALLATIONS**—In your office building, apartment building or other public location, collaborate with friends and colleagues to create and maintain a beautiful soil installation. Growing plants, a water feature and natural daylight will enhance the vitality of that special space—and will increase creativity, energy, joy and enthusiasm!

4. **VISIT ORGANIC FARMS AND FORESTS**—Coordinate timing, transportation, and simple logistics to help groups of friends, families and neighbors meet-up and journey together to special soil sanctuaries nearby.

5. **ESTABLISH COMMUNITY COMPOST PROGRAMS**—These are especially needed for office buildings, schools and other commercial facilities. Help teach your colleagues and co-workers how to become soil stewards by simply setting the intention, paying attention and ensuring proper placement of well-marked bins!

6. **ORGANIZE TREE PLANTING PARTIES**—Beautify landscapes, encourage healthy, moderate out-door activity, reverse climate change and build community by planting trees together! Choose appropriate seasons and species best suited for your region and planting zone!

7. **ORGANIZE SOIL BUILDING FLASH MOB PARTIES**—Like Soil Building Parties, these Flash Mob events are all about getting together to build soil—but are a bit more theatrical and intense in seeking to accomplish a whole lot in a relatively short period of time. These are equal parts coordination and perspiration and will be an excellent cause for celebration once completed!

SOIL—AN ALCHEMY OF LOVE

*"We know more about the movement of celestial bodies
than about the soil underfoot."*
—Leonardo Da Vinci

*"The soil is faithful to its trust: whatever you have sown in it you reap the same.
But until springtime brings the touch of God, the soil does not reveal its secrets."*
—Rumi

As we excel in our quest to become expert practitioners of THRIVING and SUSTAINABILITY, masterful mentors of the Soil Stewardship Guild, and powerful stewards of our *oikos*, our connection with soil is both foundational and quintessential. It is the starting point, and it is the goal. It is the alpha and the omega of our journey.

OIKOS (Οἶκος) is from the Ancient Greek, and means "home." It is the etymological root from which we derive the "eco" of both "ecology" and "economy." The words economy and ecology essentially mean the same thing—the practice of taking care of our home.

The most intelligent, sophisticated and advanced THRIVING practices require us to have a direct connection and relationship with living soil. This is not optional. This is essential. In addition to the food we eat, water we drink, physical movement, connection with nature, and wele (well-being) practices of mindfulness, conscious breathing, compassion and gratitude; our direct and intentional connection with the living soil is the *essential nexus* of powerful personal alchemy and planetary stewardship. It is at this nexus with soil that our bodies, minds and spirits are simultaneously *grounded*—quite literally—and *elevated*—also quite literally. It is at this point of our contact and connection with the crumbly, aromatic, living soil—each handful teaming with billions of individual living organisms—that we become the direct conduit between the above and the below. Can you imagine how many organisms are alive and at work planet-wide right now? The numbers are staggering, and carry our thoughts and imaginations into the realm of sacred inspiration. This is the fundamental, foundational source and well-spring of human life on our planet Earth. Through our awareness of this awesome truth, our consciousness can transform us—each one of us—into a pillar of love, gratitude and stewardship. We bring ourselves—

our minds, bodies and spirits—into balance and wholeness. Thus we will cultivate and embody a humble human holiness, directly connected with the vibrating life force that animates the entire universe and all life on Earth.

There is a very real and powerful alchemy in soil. Many of our ancient traditions speak of the elements: earth, air, fire and water. Where else do we have the opportunity to physically touch and hold all of these elements working together? In a handful of living soil, we find the earth minerals, moistened and enlivened with water, billions of organisms breathing the air in and out, and the fire of sunlight—of energy—flowing throughout these small, magical communities. The four elements are found in balance in healthy living soil. But there's more. Our alchemical traditions speak of a fifth element—the *quintessence*—which represents our *loving relationship* with this soil. This quintessence is a spiritual cultivation of our willful intention and deliberate action to serve as stewards, to help regenerate and heal, and to maintain an ongoing commitment to care and sustainability. The fifth element is made manifest and amplified by us humans. It is at the core of our sacred stewardship mission.

What a miraculous, regenerative, life-giving and healing process we each have the ability to engage in! This is something we can do at virtually any age—from the youngest of children and grandchildren to elders at all stages of aging. This is our birthright, and it is essential to our survival. Let us engage in the alchemy of life on Earth and build soil together!

Fire   Air

Water   Earth

ENVISION

Envision a global movement—including you, me and millions of others—mobilizing and scaling soil-building and soil-stewardship activities in communities all over the planet.

Envision thousands of communities all over the world with active, vibrant Soil Stewardship Guilds.

REFLECTIONS & QUESTIONS

➡ What daily practice will you choose to connect with soil?

➡ What soil stewardship activity are you most excited to get started with?

➡ What soil stewardship activity do you plan to do on a weekly basis?

➡ What group activity are you most excited to experience?

➡ Is there a group activity you would like to lead?

Envision soil installations and sanctuaries in homes, neighborhoods, the lobbies of apartment and office buildings—everywhere we humans live, work and play!

Envision so much of this materializing over the course of *the next five years*—and continuing thereafter for generations—an utter transformation of self, community and culture toward our shared vision of regeneration, stewardship and global sustainability.

Envision the greatest party—with sacred ceremony, delightful celebration, ample play and thoughtful experimentation—that our species has ever shared together here on Earth.

"Let us cultivate our garden!"
—Voltaire

SOIL STEWARDSHIP PLEDGE

I, _____ , believe that my connection with living soil is sacred. I promise to be a faithful steward of soil, and thus of Mother Earth—through my direct interactions with soil as well as the indirect influences of my personal choices and consumer demand. I promise to be mindful of my impact upon soil every day. I will compost all of my organic kitchen scraps and food waste. I will grow plants inside and a garden outside. I will touch soil with my hands every day. I will gently and joyfully encourage others to join this Soil Stewardship Guild. I will do all that I can to establish living soil installations at home, at work and elsewhere in my community. I understand that soil-building is a powerful way to reverse climate change. I understand that healthy, vibrant soil is key to nourishing food and clean water. I know that our existence as humans is dependent on soil. I vow to be an excellent soil steward and to help others to do the same.

_____
Sign

_____
Date

FIDES VIVI HUMUS
(Faith in Living Soil)

NOTES

1   The Soil Stewardship Guild—a Y on Earth Community program, is sometimes referred to by the letters "SSG" and is sometimes simply called the "Guild" for short.

2   As the table above indicates, Earth's ocean contains an enormous amount of carbon—dissolved in the water and taken up by phytoplankton and other life in the water. Although the ocean contains far more carbon than even terrestrial soil, the increased loading of carbon in the ocean causes acidification, making that aqueous environment dangerously toxic to marine life. It is through soil-building that we will reduce atmospheric carbon and relieve acidification pressure in the ocean. Interesting to note, the lithosphere—with rocks like calcium carbonate—contains at least 75,000,000 billion tons of carbon!

3   Visit www.yonearth.world to find biochar, wormcastings compost tea, bokashi and biodynamic soil preparation resources!

4   Visit www.fungiperfecti.com to get garden giant spawn to plant in your garden!

REFERENCES

Ackerman-Leist, Philip. *Rebuilding the Foodshed: How to Create Local, Sustainable, and Secure Food Systems.* White River Junction, VT: Chelsea Green Publishing, 2013.

Adenipekun, C.O. and R. Lawal. "Uses of Mushrooms in Bioremediation: A Review." Department of Botany, University of Ibadan. Ibadan, Nigeria, June 14, 2012. http://www. academicjournals.org/article/article1380187476_Adenipekun%20and%20Lawal.pdf.

Albrecht, William. *Soil Fertility and Animal Health.* Webster City, IA, 1958.

———. *Soil reaction (pH) and Balanced Plant Nutrition: More Evidence of the Importance of the Element Calcium in the Soil in Connection with (Cationic) Balanced Plant Nutrition, Irrespective of Humid or Arid Soils.* 1967.

Alexander, Christopher. *The Nature of Order, Book 2—The Process of Creating Life: An Essay on the Art of Building and the Nature of the Universe.* Berkeley, CA: Center for Environmental Structure, 2002.

———. *The Nature of Order, Book 1—The Phenomenon of Life: An Essay on the Art of Building and the Nature of the Universe.* Berkeley, CA: Center for Environmental Structure, 2002.

Altieri, Miguel. *Agroecology: The Science of Sustainable Agriculture.* London: IT Publications, 1998.

American College of Physicians. "American College of Physicians Issues Urgent Call to Action on Climate Change to Avert Major Threat to Public Health." Philadelphia: *ACP Online*, Apr. 19, 2016. https://www.acponline.org/acp-newsroom/climate-change-threat.

American Institutes for Research (AIR). "Effects of Outdoor Education Programs for Children in California." Palo Alto, CA, 2005. Cited by Price-Mitchell. *Psychology Today*, op. cit.

Anger, Judith and Dr. Immo Fiebrig and Martin Schnyder. *Edible Cities: Urban Permaculture for Gardens, Balconies, Rooftops, and Beyond.* White River Junction, VT: Chelsea Green Pub., 2013.

Appelhof, Mary. *Worms Eat My Garbage: How to Set Up and Maintain a Worm Composting System, 2nd Edition*. White River Junction, VT: Chelsea Green Pub., 2016 (Forthcoming).

Arava Institute for Environmental Studies. Kibbutz Ketura, Israel. http://arava.org/.

Backyard Gardening Blog. "How to Grow Amaranth." http://www.gardeningblog.net/how-to-grow/amaranth/. Accessed 1.24.17.

Bacon, Francis. "Of Gardens." In *Essays and New Atlantis*. Roslyn, N.Y.: Walter J. Black, Inc. Published for the *Classics Club*, 1942.

Bailey, Liberty Hyde. *The Holy Earth: Toward a New Environmental Ethic*. New York: Charles Scribner's Sons, 1915. New York: Christian Rural Fellowship, 1943 version republished w/ introduction by Norman Wirzba, Mineola, N.Y.: Dover Publications, 2009.

Barbut, Monique, et al. "The Ripple Effect: A Fresh Approach to Reducing Drought Impacts and Building Resilience." *United Nations Convention to Combat Desertification*. July 27, 2016. http://www.unccd.int/Lists/SiteDocumentLibrary/Publications/2016_Drought_ENG.pdf. Accessed 9.13.16.

Benenson, Bill, Eugene Rosow, Eleonore Dailly, Linda Post, Laurie Benenson, Jamie Lee Curtis, Vandana Shiva, et al. *Dirt!: The Movie*. 2010.

Bergland, Christopher. "The Power of Awe: A Sense of Wonder Promotes Loving-Kindness— Being In Awe of Something Greater than Oneself Promotes Prosocial Behavior." *Psychology Today*. May 20, 2015. https://www.psychologytoday.com/blog/the-athletes-way/201505/the-power-awe-sense-wonder-promotes-loving-kindness.

Bernhard, Toni. "4 Tips for Slowing Down to Reduce Stress." *Psychology Today*. Sept. 13, 2011. https://www.psychologytoday.com/blog/turning-straw-gold/201109/4-tips-slowing-down-reduce-stress.

Berry, Thomas with Thomas Clarke, SJ. *Befriending the Earth: A Theology of Reconciliation Between Humans and the Earth*. Mystic, CT: Twenty-Third Publications, 1991.

Berry, Thomas. *The Christian Future and the Fate of Earth*. Maryknoll, New York: Orbis Books, 2009.

———. *The Great Work: Our Way Into the Future*. New York: Bell Tower, 1999.

———. *A Place on Earth*. New York: Harcourt, Brace and World, 1967.

———. *Collected Poems*. San Francisco: North Point Press, 1985.

———. *The Unsettling of America: Culture and Agriculture.* San Francisco: Sierra Club Books, 1986.

———. *To What Listens.* Crete, NE: Best Cellar Press, 1975.

———. *What Are People For?* San Francisco: North Point Press, 1990.

Bonsall, Will. *Will Bonsall's Essential Guide to Radical, Self-Reliant Gardening: Innovative Techniques for Growing Vegetables, Grains, and Perennial Food Crops with Minimal Fossil Fuel and Animal Inputs.* White River Junction, VT: Chelsea Green, 2015.

Bornstein, Robert. "Observations of the Urban Heat Island Effect in New York City." New York: New York University. 1968. http://journals.ametsoc.org/doi/pdf/10.1175/15200450(1968)007%3C0575%3AOOTUHI%3E2.0.CO%3B2. Accessed 12.12.16.

Breysse, Patrick, Gregory Diette, Elizabeth Matsui, Arlene Butz, Nadia Hansel and Meredith McCormack. "Indoor Air Pollution and Asthma in Children." *PubMed.* US National Library of Medicine, National Institutes of Health. 7(2): 102-106. May 1, 2010. https://www.ncbi.nlm.nih.gov/pmc/articles/PMC3266016/. Accessed 12.12.16.

Buettner, Dan. *Blue Zones: Lessons for Living Longer From the People Who've Lived the Longest.* Washington, D.C.: National Geographic, 2008.

———. *Thrive: Finding Happiness the Blue Zones Way.* Washington, D.C.: National Geographic, 2010.

Capra, Fritjof. "Laudato Si': The Ecological Ethics and Systemic Thought of Pope Francis." June 22, 2015. http://www.fritjofcapra.net/laudato-si-the-ecological-ethics-and-systemic-thought-of-pope-francis/.

———. *The Hidden Connections: Integrating the Biological, Cognitive, and Social Dimensions of Life Into a Science of Sustainability.* New York: Doubleday, 2002.

———. *The Web of Life: A New Scientific Understanding of Living Systems.* New York: Anchor Books, 1996.

Center for Climate and Energy Solutions. "Global Anthropogenic GHG Emissions by Sector." Diagrams and charts. http://www.c2es.org/facts-figures/international-emissions. Accessed 11.6.16.

Coleman, Elliot. *Four Season Harvest: Organic Vegetables from Your Home Garden All Year Around.* White River Junction, VT: Chelsea Green, 1999.

Crawford, Martin. *Trees for Gardens, Orchards and Permaculture.* White River Junction, VT: Chelsea Green Pub., 2015.

Creasy, Rosalind with Cathy Wilkinson Barash. "Edible Landscaping: Grow $700 of Food in 100 Square Feet!" *Mother Earth News*. Dec. 2009/Jan. 2010.

Dalai Lama XIV, The. "A Question of Our Own Survival." In *Moral Ground: Ethical Action for a Planet in Peril*. Forward by Desmond Tutu. San Antonio, TX: Trinity University Press, 2010.

———. *Transforming the Mind: Teachings on Generating Compassion*. London: Thorsons Publishing Group, 2000.

Deppe, Carol. *The Tao of Vegetable Gardening: Cultivating Tomatoes, Greens, Peas, Beans, Squash, Joy, and Serenity*. White River Junction, VT: Chelsea Green Pub., 2015.

Despommier, Dickson. *The Vertical Farm: Feeding the World in the 21st Century*. New York: St. Martin's Press, 2010.

Diamond, Jared M. *Collapse: How Societies Choose to Fail or Succeed*. New York: Viking, 2005.

Earth's CO2 Home Page. https://www.co2.earth//. Accessed 9.7.16.

Eden Projects. "Plant Trees. Save Lives." www.edenprojects.org. Accessed 11.30.16.

Eliades, Angelo. "Lessons from an Urban Back Yard Food Forest Experiment." *Permaculture Research Institute*. Apr. 13, 2011. http://permaculturenews.org/2011/04/13/lessons-from-an-urban-back-yard-food-forest-experiment/.

Emerson, Ralph Waldo. *Nature*. Croton Falls, NY: Spiral Press, 1932.

Ernest, Danielle. "10 Superfoods You Can Grow In Your Backyard." *Better Homes and Gardens*. http://www.bhg.com/gardening/vegetable/vegetables/10-superfoods-you-can-grow/ Publish date unknown. Accessed 11.16.15.

Farmland LP. "One Acre Feeds a Person." Online: *Farmland LP: Investing in Sustainability*. Posted by Jason Bradford. Jan. 13, 2012. http://www.farmlandlp.com/2012/01/one-acre-feeds-a-person/

FEWresources.org. "Losing Ground: Re-Thinking Soil as a Renewal Resource." http://www.fewresources.org/soil-science-and-society-were-running-out-of-dirt.html. Accessed 9.7.16.

Finley, Ron. "A Guerilla Gardener in South Central LA." Ted Talk. Feb, 2013. http://www.ted.com/talks/ron_finley_a_guerilla_gardener_in_south_central_la?language=en. Accessed 11.30.16.

Finley, Ron. "The Gangsta Gardener—A Ron Finley Project." www.ronfinley.com. Accessed 11.30.16.

Fisher, Adrian Ayres. "Why Not Start Today: Backyard Carbon Sequestration Is Something Nearly Everyone Can Do." *Resilience: Building a World of Resilient Communities*. Sept. 2, 2015.

Flores, H.C., with forward by Toby Hemenway and illustrations by Jackie Holmstrom. *Food Not Lawns: How to Turn Your Yard Into a Garden and Your Neighborhood Into a Community*. White River Junction, VT: Chelsea Green, 2006.

Food and Agriculture Organization (FAO) of the United Nations. "Food Loss and Food Waste." http://www.fao.org/food-loss-and-food-waste/en/. Accessed 8.12.16.

Fraser, Evan and Andrew Rimas. *Empires of Food: Feast, Famine and the Rise and Fall of Civilizations*. London: Random House Books, 2010.

Freeman, David. "Why You Should NEVER Throw Old Clothes in The Trash." *Huffington Post*. Oct 7, 2016. http://www.huffingtonpost.com/entry/why-trashing-old-clothes-is-so-bad-for-the-environment_us_57f408f1e4b015995f2b93cb?section=&.

Friedman, Thomas "The World's Hot Spot." *New York Times*. August, 19 2015.

Fukuoka, Masanobu. *One-Straw Revolution: An Introduction to Natural Farming*. New York: New York Review Books, 2009.

———. *Sowing Seeds in the Desert: Natural Farming, Global Restoration, and Ultimate Food Security*. White River Junction, VT: Chelsea Green, 2012.

Fuller, R. Buckminster. *Operating Manual for Spaceship Earth*. Carbondale: Southern Illinois University Press, 1969.

Garden Mentors. "Protein-Rich Plants for the Vegetable Garden." Jun 8, 2010. http://gardenmentors.com/garden-help/grow-your-ownfood/protein-rich-plants-for-the-vegetable-garden/

Gellman, Lindsay and Rachel Feintzeig. "Social Seal of Approval Lures Talent: Employers Tout Their B Corp Label as a Credential to Compete for Young Hires" *The Wall Street Journal*. November 12, 2013.

Gifford, Dawn. *Sustainability Starts at Home: how to Save Money While Saving the Planet*. Small Footprint Family Publishing, 2013. http://www.smallfootprintfamily.com/.

Glausiusz, Josie. "Is Dirt the New Prozac?" *Discover Magazine*, June 14, 2007.

Good Earth Publications. Various resources re: keeping chickens, gardening, "Occupy Backyards." http://www.goodearthpublications.com/.

Goodall, Jane. *Seeds of Hope: Wisdom and Wonder from the World of Plants*. New York: Grand Central Publishing, 2013.

Grace, Stephen. *Grow: Stories from the Urban Food Movement*. Bozeman, MT: Bangtail Press, 2015.

Grodnitzky, Gustavo. *Culture Trumps Everything: The Unexpected Truth about the Ways Environment Changes Biology, Psychology, and Behavior*. Mountain Frog Publishing, 2014.

Hawken, Paul. *Blessed Unrest: How the Largest Movement in the World Came Into Being and Why No One Saw It Coming*. New York: Viking Press, 2007.

———. *Drawdawn: The Most Comprehensive Plan Ever Proposed to Reverse Global Warming*. New York: Penguin Books, 2017.

Hayes, Shannon. *Radical Homemakers: Reclaiming Domesticity from a Consumer Culture*. Richmondville, NY: Left to Write Press, 2010.

Held, Stephanie. "10 Detroit Urban Farms Rooting Goodness Into the City." *Daily Detroit*. July 6, 2015. http://www.dailydetroit.com/2015/07/06/10-detroit-urban-farms-rooting-goodness-into-the-city/. Accessed 9.9.16.

Henderson, Hazel. "Gross National Happiness." In Dawson Church, et al., editors. *Einstein's Business: Engaging Soul, Imagination, and Excellence in the Workplace*. Santa Rosa, CA: Elite Books, 2005.

Hemenway, Toby. *Gaia's Garden: A Guide to Home-scale Permaculture*, 2nd ed. White River Junction, VT: Chelsea Green Publishing Company, 2009.

———. *The Permaculture City: Regenerative Design for Urban, Suburban, and Town Resilience*. White River Junction, VT: Chelsea Green Pub., 2015.

Hesterman, Oran. *Fair Food: Growing A Healthy, Sustainable Food System for All*. New York: Public Affairs, 2011.

Howard, Brian Clark. "Connecting With Nature Boosts Creativity and Health: Richard Louv Explains How Society Can Overcome Nature-Deficit-Disorder." *National Geographic*. June 30, 2013. http://news.nationalgeographic.com/news/2013/06/130628-richard-louv-nature-deficit-disorder-health-environment/.

Hrala, Josh. "Looking at Trees Can Reduce Your Stress Levels, Even In the Middle of a City." *Science Alert*. May 8, 2016. http://www.sciencealert.com/urban-tree-coverage-can-significantly-reduce-stress-study-finds. Accessed 8.15.16.

Independent. "The Human Brain is the Most Complex Structure in the Universe. Let's Do All We Can to Unravel Its Mysteries." April 2, 2014. http://www.independent.co.uk/voices/editorials/the-human-brain-is-the-most-complex-structure-in-the-universe-let-s-do-all-we-can-to-unravel-its-9233125.html.

Ingham, Elaine and Carole Ann Rollins. *10 Steps to Gardening with Nature.* Corvalis, OR: Sustainable Studies Institute, 2011.

Ingham, Elaine. *Soil Biology Primer.* Ankeny, IA: Soil and Water Conservation Society, 2000.

———. Website Resource. www.soilfoodweb.com

Jackson, Wes. *Consulting the Genius of the Place: An Ecological Approach to a New Agriculture.* Berkeley, CA: Counterpoint, 2010.

Ji, Sayer and Keith Bell. "Is Industrial Farming Destroying Rain-Making Bacteria?" *GreenMedInfo.* July 27, 2015. http://www.greenmedinfo.com/blog/california-drought-surprising-cause. Accessed 11.14.16.

Jung, Carl Gustav. *The Earth Has a Soul: C.G. Jung on Nature, Technology and Modern Life.* Berkeley, CA: North Atlantic Books, 2002.

Kaplan, Sarah. "A Surprising Simple Solution to Bad Indoor Air Quality: Potted Plants." *The Washington Post.* Aug. 24, 2016. https://www.washingtonpost.com/news/speaking-of-science/wp/2016/08/24/a-surprising-simple-solution-to-bad-indoor-air-quality-potted-plants/?hpid=hp_weekend-chain_sos-feature%3Ahomepage%2Fstory.

Koohafkan, Parviz and Miguel Altieri. *Forgotten Agricultural Heritage: Reconnecting Food Systems and Sustainable Development.* Earthscan Food and Agriculture Series, Oxford, UK: Taylor and Francis Group, 2016.

Korn, Larry. *One-Straw Revolutionary: The Philosophy and Work of Masanobu Fukuoka.* White River Junction, VT: Chelsea Green Pub., 2015.

Korten, David. *The Great Turning: From Empire to Earth Community.* San Francisco, CA: Berrett-Koehler; Bloomfield, CT: Kumarian Press, 2006.

Kourik, Robert. *Understanding Roots: Discover How to Make Your Garden Flourish.* White River Junction, VT: Chelsea Green Pub., 2015.

Kramer, Arthur and Kirk Erickson. "Capitalizing on Cortical Plasticity: Influence of Physical Activity on Cognition and Brain Function." *Science Direct.* Vol. 11, No. 8. Avail. Online July 12, 2007. http://dericbownds.net/uploaded_images/kramer.pdf.

Krupnick, Ellie. "How to Turn Off Your Phone, Shut Down Your Computer and Totally Unplug Every Single Week." *Huffington Post.* March 11, 2014.

Lidsky, Isaac. "What Reality Are You Creating for Yourself?" TedTalk. June, 2016. https://www.ted.com/talks/isaac_lidsky_what_reality_are_you_creating_for_yourself?language=en#t-37588. Accessed 11.8.16.

Lloyd, Janice. "'Blue Zones' Author: 9 Secrets to Live a Long Life." *USA Today.* November 4, 2012.

Logsdon, Gene. *A Sanctuary of Trees: Beechnuts, Birdsongs, Baseball Bats, and Benedictions.* White River Junction, VT: Chelsea Green Pub., 2012.

Lott, Melissa C. "UN Says That if Food Waste was a Country, It'd be the #3 Global Greenhouse Gas Emitter." *Scientific American.* Sept. 12, 2013. http://blogs.scientificamerican.com/plugged-in/un-says-that-if-food-waste-was-a-country-ite28099d-be-the-3-global-greenhouse-gas-emitter/. Accessed 9.20.16.

Louv, Richard. *Last Child in the Woods: Saving Our Children From Nature Deficit Disorder.* Chapel Hill, NC: Algonquin Books of Chapel Hill. 2008.

———. *Nature Principle: Reconnecting with Life in A Virtual Age.* Chapel Hill, N.C.: Algonquin Books of Chapel Hill, 2012.

Lovelock, James. *Gaia: A New Look at Life on Earth.* Oxford; New York: Oxford University Press, 1979.

Lyons, Oren. "Keepers of Life." In *Moral Ground: Ethical Action for a Planet in Peril.* Forward by Desmond Tutu. San Antonio, TX: Trinity University Press, 2010.

Maathai, Wangari. *The Greenbelt Movement: Sharing the Approach and the Experience.* New York: Lantern Books, 2006.

Macnamara, Looby. *7 Ways to Think Differently: Embrace Potential, Respond to Life, Discover Abundance.* White River Junction, VT: Chelsea Green Pub., 2014.

Main, Emily. "The 12 Most Toxic Chemicals in Your Home: Learn What You're Being Exposed to– and How to Protect Yourself." *Prevention Magazine.* Nov. 4, 2013. http://www.prevention.com/health/healthy-living/top-12-endocrine-disrupting-chemicals-in-your-home. Accessed 10.20.16.

McGrane, Sally. "German Forest Ranger Finds That Trees Have Social Networks, Too." *New York Times,* Jan. 29, 2016.

McIntosh, Alastair. *Soil and Soul: People versus Corporate Power*. London: Aurum Press, 2001.

McKibben, Bill. *Earth: Making A Life On A Tough New Planet*. New York: Time Books, 2010.

Miller, Kenneth. "How Mushrooms Can Save the World: Crusading Mycologist
Paul Stamets Says Fungi Can Clean Up Everything from Oil Spills to Nuclear
Meltdowns." *Discover Magazine*. May 31, 2013. http://discovermagazine.com/2013/
julyaug/13-mushrooms-clean-up-oil-spills-nuclear-meltdowns-and-human-health.

Mollison, Bill and Reny Mia Slay. *Introduction to Permaculture*. Tyalgum Australia: Tagari
Publications, 1992.

———. *Permaculture: A Designers' Manual*. Tasmania, Australia: Tagari Publications, 1997.

———. *A Practical Guide for a Sustainable Future*. Washington, D.C.: Island Press, 1990.

Mooney, Chris. "U.S. Scientists Officially Declare 2016 the Hottest Year on Record. That Makes
Three In a Row." *Washington Post*. January 18, 2017. https://www.washingtonpost.com/news/
energy-environment/wp/2017/01/18/u-s-scientists-officially-declare-2016-the-hottest-year-
on-record-that-makes-three-in-a-row/?utm_term=.b8cf218cd3bb.

Nabhan, Gary Paul. "Heirloom Chile Peppers and Climate Change." In *Moral Ground: Ethical
Action for a Planet in Peril*. Forward by Desmond Tutu. San Antonio, TX: Trinity University
Press, 2010.

Nadworny, Elissa and Cory Turner. "How A Great Teacher Cultivates Veggies (And Kids) In
The Bronx" (RE: Teacher Stephen Ritz). *National Public Radio*. January 19, 2016.

Nearing, Helen. *Living the Good Life: How to Live Sanely and Simply in a Troubled World*. New
York: Schocken Books, 1970.

Orr, David. *Hope is an Imperative: The Essential David Orr*. Washington, D.C.: Island Press,
2011.

Otto, Stella. *The Backyard Orchardist: A Complete Guide to Growing Fruit Trees in the Home
Garden, 2nd Edition*. White River Junction, VT: Chelsea Green Pub., 2015.

Pershouse, Didi. *The Ecology of Care: Medicine, Agriculture, Money, and the Quiet Power of
Human and Microbial Communities*. Thetford Center, VT: Mycelium Books, 2016.

Petrini, Carlo, William McCuaig and Alice Waters. *Slow Food: The Case for Taste*. New York:
Columbia University Press, 2003.

Pimentel, David. "Soil Erosion: A Food and Environmental Threat." *Journal of the Environment, Development and Sustainability*. Vol. 8, 2006.

Pollan, Michael. *Botany of Desire: A Plant's Eye View of the World*. New York: Random House, 2001.

Pope Francis. *Laudato Si': Encyclical on Climate Change and Inequality: On Care For Our Common Home*. Brooklyn, NY: Melville House Publishing, 2015.

Price-Mitchell, PhD., Marilyn. "Does Nature Make Us Happy? Connection with Nature are Linked to Happiness and Ecological Sustainability." *Psychology Today*. Mar 27, 2014. https://www.psychologytoday.com/blog/the-moment-youth/201403/does-nature-make-us-happy. Accessed 8.24.16.

Ritz, Stephen. "A Teacher Growing Green in the South Bronx." *TEDxManhattan*. February, 2012. https://www.ted.com/talks/stephen_ritz_a_teacher_growing_green_in_the_south_bronx.

Rollins, Carole Ann PhD, Elaine Ingham. *10 Steps to Gardening with Nature: Using Sustainable Steps to Replicate Mother Nature*. Novato, CA: Gardening With Nature, 2011.

Roseboro, Ken. "Why Is Glyphosate Sprayed on Crops Right Before Harvest?" *EcoWatch*. Mar. 5, 2016. http://www.ecowatch.com/why-is-glyphosate-sprayed-on-crops-right-before-harvest-1882187755.html. Accessed 9.15.16.

Roszak, Theodore. *Ecopsychology: Restoring the Earth, Healing the Mind*. Berkeley, CA: Counterpoint, 1995.

Salatin, Joel. *Folks, This Ain't Normal: A Farmer's Advice for Happier Hens, Healthier People, and a Better World*. New York: Center Street, 2011.

———. *The Sheer Ecstasy of Being a Lunatic Farmer*. Swoope, VA: Polyface Publishing, 2010.

Sanders, Noah. *Born-Again Dirt: Farming to the Glory of God; Cultivating a Biblical Vision for God-Glorifying Agriculture*. Sand Springs, OK: Rora Valley Publishing, 2013.

Savory, Allan. *Holistic Management Handbook: Healthy Land, Healthy Profits*. Washington D.C.: Island Press. 1999.

———. "How to Fight Desertification and Reverse Climate Change." TedTalk. https://www.ted.com/talks/allan_savory_how_to_green_the_world_s_deserts_and_reverse_climate_change?language=en. Filmed Feb, 2013.

Savory Institute. "Restoring The Climate Through Capture and Storage of Soil Carbon Through Holistic Planned Grazing." White paper, 2015. http://savory.global/assets/docs/evidence-apers/RestoringClimateWhitePaper2015.pdf. Accessed 9.14.16.

Schlossberg, Tatiana. "English Village Becomes Climate Leader by Quietly Cleaning Up Its Own Patch." *New York Times.* Aug. 21, 2016. http://www.nytimes.com/2016/08/22/science/english-village-becomes-climate-leader-by-quietly-cleaning-up-its-own-patch.html?mwrsm=Email&_r=0. Accessed 8.21.16.

Schwartz, Judith. *Cows Save the Planet: And Other Improbable Ways of Restoring Soil to Health the Earth.* White River Junction, VT: Chelsea Green Pub., 2013.

———. "Soil as Carbon Storehouse: New Weapon in Climate Fight?" *Environment 360.* Yale. Mar. 4, 2014. http://e360.yale.edu/feature/soil_as_carbon_storehouse_new_weapon_in_climate_fight/2744/. Accessed 9.7.16.

Shiva, Vandana. *Soil Not Oil: Environmental Justice in an Age of Climate Crisis.* Berkeley, CA: North Atlantic Books, 2015.

Smith, Libby. "Cooperative Offers Solution In West Denver Food Desert." CBS Denver. July 7, 2015. http://denver.cbslocal.com/2015/07/07/cooperative-offers-solution-in-west-denver-food-desert/. Accessed 9.9.16.

Soil Solution to Climate Change. Dir. by Carol Hirashima and Jill Cloutier. Perf. Kelly Smith. 2011.

The Soil Story. Dir. Englehart, Ryland. YouTube Video. Published by Kiss the Ground, Aug. 31, 2015. https://www.youtube.com/watch?v=nvAoZ14cP7Q. Accessed 5.27.16.

Stamets, Paul. *Mycelium Running: How Mushrooms Can Help Save the World.* Berkeley: Ten Speed Press, 2005.

———. *Mushroom Cultivator: A Practical Guide to Growing Mushrooms at Home.* Olympia, WA: Agarikon Press; Seattle, WA: Western Distribution, 1983.

Steffen, Alex. "A Talk Given at a Conservation Meeting a Hundred Years from Now." Online: http://www.alexsteffen.com/future_conservation_meeting_talk, 12.12.2015.

Suttie, Jill. "How Nature Can Make You Kinder, Happier, and More Creative. Greater Good: The Science of a Meaningful Life." University of California, Berkeley. Mar 2, 2016. http://greatergood.berkeley.edu/article/item/how_nature_makes_you_kinder_happier_more_creative. Accessed 8.24.16.

Suzuki, David. *The Legacy: An Elder's Vision for Our Sustainable Future.* Vancouver, BC: Greystone Books, 2010.

———. *Sacred Balance: Rediscovering Our Place in Nature.* Vancouver, BC: Greystone, 1997.

Symphony of the Soil. Directed and Written by Deborah Koons, Perf. Ignacio Chapela, Vandana Shiva, Elaine Ingham. 2013.

Tasch, Woody. *Slow Money: Investing as if Food, Farms, and Fertility Mattered.* White River Junction, VT: Chelsea Green Pub., 2008.

Thich Nhat Hanh. *How to Eat.* Berkeley, CA: Parallax Press, 2015.

———. *How to Love.* Berkeley, CA: Parallax Press, 2015.

———. *How to Relax.* Berkeley, CA: Parallax Press, 2015.

Thompson, William I. "The Meta Industrial Village." *Darkness and Scattered Light: Four Talks on the Future.* Garden City, NY: Anchor Press, 1978.

Toensmeier, Eric. *The Carbon Farming Solution: A Global Toolkit of Perennial Crops and Regenerative Agriculture Practices for Climate Change Mitigation and Food Security.* White River Junction, VT: Chelsea Green Pub., 2016.

Tompkins, Peter and Christopher Bird. *Secret Life of Plants.* New York: Harper & Row, 1973.

———. *Secrets of the Soil.* New York: Harper & Row, 1989.

Tutu, Archbishop Desmond. "Forward," In *Moral Ground: Ethical Action for a Planet in Peril.* Forward by Desmond Tutu. San Antonio, TX: Trinity University Press, 2010.

UNEP International Soil Reference and Information Centre (ISRIC). World Atlas of Desertification, 1997. http://www.grida.no/graphicslib/detail/degraded-soils_c4c4.

Union of Concerned Scientists. "Plant the Plate: We all know it—we should eat more fruits and vegetables." Online: *Union of Concerned Scientists: Science for a Healthy Planet and Safer World.* http://www.ucsusa.org/food_and_agriculture/solutions/expand-healthy-food-access/plant-the-plate.html#.Vkq9D7-HzgU. Accessed 1.24.17.

United Nations Conference on Trade and Development. "Wake Up Before It Is Too Late: Make Agriculture Truly Sustainable Now For Food Security in a Changing Climate." UNCTAD Report 2013. http://unctad.org/en/PublicationsLibrary/ditcted2012d3_en.pdf.

Urban Jungle. "Vertical Green Walls" http://www.urbanjunglephila.com/verticalgardens.html. Accessed 12.12.16.

US Environmental Protection Agency. "Indoor Air Quality." https://cfpub.epa.gov/roe/chapter/air/indoorair.cfm. Accessed 12.12.16.

Vita, Ietef a.k.a. DJ CAVEM MOETEVATION. The Produce Section: The Harvest. Music Album. http://djcavem.com/the-produce-section-the-harvest/. Accessed 9.9.16.

Waldinger, Robert. "What Makes a Good Life? Lessons from the Longest Study on Happiness." TEDxBeaconStreet. Nov 2015. Harvard Study of Adult Development. https://www.ted.com/talks/robert_waldinger_what_makes_a_good_life_lessons_from_the_logest_study_on_happiness?language=en. Accessed 6.8.16.

Walsh, Bryan. "Getting Real About the High Price of Cheap Food." *Time.* Aug 21, 2009.

Walter, Robin. "Small is Beautiful but Beautiful is not Small: An Interview with Scott Pittman and Durga" *Huffington Post.* Nov. 1, 2016. http://www.huffingtonpost.com/entry/small-is-beautiful-but-beautiful-is-not-small-an-interview_us_5818da99e4b096e870696b95. Accessed 11.16.16.

Weil, M.D., Dr. Andrew. *Spontaneous Happiness: A New Path to Emotional Well-Being.* New York: Little, Brown and Co., 2011.

———. *Spontaneous Healing: How to Discover and Embrace Your Body's Natural Ability to Maintain and Heal Itself.* New York: Random House, 1995.

Weisman, Alan *Gaviotas: A Village to Reinvent the World.* White River Junction, VT: Chelsea Green Pub., 1998.

White, Courtney. *Grass, Soil, Hope: A Journey Through Carbon Country.* White River Junction, VT: Chelsea Green Pub., 2014.

———. *Two Percent Solutions for the Planet: 50 Low-Cost, Low-=Tech, Nature-Based Practices for Combatting Hunter, Drought, and Climate Change.* White River Junction, VT: Chelsea Green Publishing, 2015.

Whitehouse, The. "Findings from the Select Federal Reports: The National Security Implications of a Changing Climate." https://www.whitehouse.gov/sites/default/files/docs/National_Security_Implications_of_Changing_Climate_Final_051915.pdf. Washington, D.C., May 2015.

Williams, Florence. "This is Your Brain on Nature." *National Geographic.* January, 2016.

Wilson, Edward O. *Biophilia.* Cambridge, MA: Harvard University Press, 1984.

Wilson, Gail, Charles Rice, Matthias Rillig, et al. "Soil Aggregation and Carbon Sequestration are Tightly Correlated with the Abundance of Arbuscular Mycorrhizal Fungi: Results from Long-Term Field Experiments." *Ecology Letters* (2009) 12: 452-461.

Wilson, Peter Lamborn, Christopher Bamford and Kevin Townley. *Green Hermeticism: Alchemy and Ecology.* Great Barrington, MA: Lindisfarne Books, 2007.

Winfrey, Oprah. *Food, Health and Happiness: 115 On-point Recipes for Great Meals and a Better Life.* New York: Melcher Media, 2017.

Zelenski, J. M., and Nisbet, E. K. "Happiness and Feeling Connected: The Distinct Role of Nature Relatedness. *Environment and Behavior.* 46(1), 3-23. 2014. Cited in Price-Mitchell, op cit.

ACKNOWLEDGEMENTS

It truly takes a village to write and publish a book! This *Soil Stewardship Handbook* is no exception and has benefited from the insights and expertise of so many dear friends and colleagues. A very special thank you to:

Adrian Del Caro
Aly Artusio-Glimpse
Amelia Vincent
Artem Nikulkov
Brad and Lindsay Lidge
Brigitte Mars
Bruce Bridges
Carol Consulman
Jake Welsh
Jed Siebert
Jeni Rinner
Jennifer Menke
Joe Brenner
Keven Townley
La'ne Saan
Maggie McLaughlin

Marcia Perry
Mark Bosco, SJ
Mark Guttridge
Marty Sugg
Meri Mullins
Michael Bowman
Michael Murphy
Moyra Stiles
Rose and Brook Le Van
Rowdy and Christi Yeatts
Seth Itzkan
Sina Simantob
Tanner Watt
Tom O'Loughlin
Travis Robinson

Y ON EARTH COMMUNITY

The Y on Earth Community is a network of diverse people and organizations who curate and lead experiences, workshops and meet-ups that transform our culture by cultivating thriving and sustainability practices. By delivering as much inspiration as information and by having loads of fun while sharing fresh, unique life-hacks, the Y on Earth Community helps people get smarter, feel better and heal the planet through simple, accessible and life-changing tools and techniques. The Y on Earth Community is a project of Regenerative Earth, a 501(c)3 non-profit organization. To learn more, to get involved and to support the Y on Earth Community, visit www.yonearthcommunity.org.

Engage with the growing Y on Earth Community and get the latest updates, content and life-hacks!

Website: yonearth.world   Facebook: facebook.com/yonearthworld/

Twitter: @yonearthworld   Meet Up: yonearthworld/meetup

Instagram: instagram.com/yonearthworld/

Help create the world we really want by supporting the Y on Earth Community, a project of Regenerative Earth, a 501(c)3 charitable organization. Your tax-deductible contribution supports the Community's work bringing the Y on Earth message of information and inspiration to schools, universities, houses of worship and other community organizations!

Contributions can be made at www.yonearthcommunity.org, or by sending checks to:

Y on Earth Community
PO Box 2333
Boulder, Colorado 80306

Thank you for your generous support!

To bring the Y on Earth experience to your community, to join our growing Community Ambassador Network of leaders, and for Speaking, Book Signing, Seminar and Curated Workshop experiences, contact us at: y@yonearth.world

ABOUT *Y ON EARTH*

Y on Earth reveals how thriving by cultivating true health and well-being is essential to creating a sustainable culture and future. This tour de force is essential reading for millennials as well as their parents, grandparents, educators and employers!

You can order copies of the eBook, audiobook and first edition printed paperback at www.yonearth.world/shop.

Here's what people are saying about *Y on Earth*:

"After my baseball career was over, I thought long and hard about my priorities, especially as a dad. Aaron asks the tough questions, but more importantly, provides the answers and the motivation toward a higher calling of responsibility toward our planet and each other. Wherever your plot, wherever your lot, it's time to make a difference!"
—Brad Lidge, 2008 World Series Champion, Philadelphia Phillies

"Y on Earth is a wise, affirming, even affable guide to reckoning with our emerging environmental crises—a topic that's usually addressed in technical or dire terms. Conversational without being preachy, the author focuses on how things work rather than what we should fear. Read it to feel less overwhelmed and more empowered."
—Judith Schwartz, author *Water in Plain Sight*

"What is the importance of beauty, balance, and listening in our daily lives? How does awe, wonder, and cooking increase our joy? How can walking, generosity, and unplugging from our technology deepen our relationships? Is there power in humility? I could go on and on about the countless colorful threads Aaron weaves together to show us how rich, rewarding, and empowering life can be if we so choose it. So dig in, dig deep, and never forget that the greatest gift you have to offer the world is a healed up, restored, peaceful and balanced you!"
—Brad Corrigan, Dispatch

"Y on Earth *is a needed read not only for Millennials but for all who want to survive—both personally and globally. The current unsustainable consumption of time, goods and the Earth's collapsing resources threatens us all.* Y on Earth *is a pleasant, easy read that assesses the systemic problems that face humanity, while offering insights and approaches to reconnect to soil, to each other and to ourselves."*

—Hunter Lovins, author, *Climate Capitalism*
and founder, Natural Capitalism Solutions

"Y on Earth *presents bridges of knowledge and wisdom over which we can travel from worldviews of scarcity, degradation and injustice towards celebrating and protecting the abundance of God's Divine Creation. It is an inspiration for humanizing our lives, and for becoming more neighborly, more purposeful, more humble and more principled in our homes and economies."*

—James Featherby, Chair, Church of England,
Ethical Investment Advisory Board and author, *Of Markets and Men*

"Y on Earth *is a timely and compelling guide to living and loving in our evermore complex and rapidly changing world. Comprehensive in its scope, it deals with almost all aspects of what it means to be a human. It explores our relationship to the earth, to other people, to our vocations, to our spirituality, to technology, to culture, and to our search for meaning in the 21st century. It is well worth reading!"*

—Dr. Ralph Sorenson, Director, Whole Foods Inc.,
and President Emeritus, Babson College

"*In a world full of abundance, it is interesting that we feel more disconnected, discontent and dis-eased than ever. In the deep thinking that is at the core of* Y on Earth, *Aaron provides a way of thinking about connectedness, contentment and ease in a manner that is both refreshing and accessible. Simply reading the chapter titles has the power to change perspective and reconnects us to the notion of choice . . . in how we live in community, family, work and this world. Our very survival could depend on living effortlessly in the midst of abundance and complexity. This is a fabulous read that must be contemplated and shared among our many connections."*

—Jandel Allen-Davis, MD

ABOUT THE AUTHOR

Aaron William Perry is a writer, public speaker, impact entrepreneur, consultant, artist and father. The author of *Y on Earth: Get Smarter, Feel Better, Heal the Planet,* Aaron works with the Y on Earth Community team and Impact Ambassadors to spread the THRIVING and SUSTAINABILITY messages of hopeful and empowering information and inspiration to diverse communities throughout the world.

He has launched companies in the recycling, renewable energy and local and organic food sectors. Aaron consults to dozens of innovative organizations, companies and entrepreneurs. An experienced business and literary writer, Aaron holds an MA in Germanistik from the University of Colorado, where he studied Philosophy, Literature, Environmental Policy and Sustainable Development. While in graduate school he spent weekends and holidays studying Permaculture and Indigenous Wisdom throughout the Rocky Mountain region. He resides in Colorado where he is continually in awe of the weather, appreciative of the singing birds, and entertained by the antics of his backyard, free-range chickens.

Made in the USA
Monee, IL
25 June 2022

9853472OR00033